From God's Heart

Photographs including cover photo by Inger Marie Nordin

Published by ROOTED Publishing
Belle River, Ontario, Canada
www.rootedpublishing.com

ISBN: 978-82-692028-4-7

From God's Heart

God has so much on His Heart for you. He wants to encourage you, challenge you and comfort you. Receive His Words for you ♥

Inger Marie Nordin

My Love

My love is flowing from my throne
It is flowing to cover you completely
Let it take away your pain
Let it take away your sorrow
Let it flow freely to all your rooms

My love brings healing
My love brings life
It gives an answer to your longings
It will tear down your fences
Let it wash away every tear you have cried

My love will set you free
My love will release the joy
You have felt so much pain
but I will give you from my heart
Let my love change your life

An Undivided Heart

Seek me from an undivided heart
Then you will find me
Call on me from the bottom of your heart
Then I will be there

For my heart is calling on yours
I miss having you close
I miss listening to your deep sighs
and telling you I love you so much

I am longing to heal you
to heal your wounds
I will fill your cup now
so that you joyfully and boldly can stand

I will throw out all confusion
I will give you my peace
I will pour out my love
on you in this place

Spring Thaw of Your Heart

Look, I am holding your heart between my hands
It has been frozen for so long
Now I want to warm it up
I will make it come alive
so that it can beat to my rhythm

Look, I am holding it so gently
Little by little it thaws
It is painful
but I am with you all the way

Your pain will turn to praise
when you see what it is to live
to live a life with me
In full harmony with who you are called to be
Who you are in me

Do not stop the process
Let me thaw you
Now it is hard, but hold on
so that you can be healed
Because healing starts with the heart
And from your heart healing will flow
to your whole being
Feel how your heart is coming alive
It is pounding in rhythm to my heartbeat
Let your ice melt in my hands
Then the melting water will become a living well
That will bring healing to you
And to the one I am sending you to

It is time to come out in freedom
Rest in me
Let me do what I must do
So that you can do what you must do

A Crushed Spirit

In the highest and most holy place I live
And in those who have a crushed spirit
In a high and holy place I am enthroned
And in those who have a humble spirit

I am calling on your heart
I am calling on your spirit
Come, let me take your pain
Come, let me take your hand

I know about your longings
I know about your wounds
Let me tear down your fences
Let me give you good conditions

You are just looking at yourself
and are digging yourself deep down
I stepped down to earth
to give you life and peace

A Crushed Heart

Do not be afraid of being crushed
It is necessary for the aroma
that is in you to come out
Let yourself be crushed, let it happen
so that my beautiful aroma can get through

My aroma will call forth people to me via you
Let me do my work in you
Let me finish my job – be crushed
Because I live in a crushed heart
There I raise my throne
There I reveal my glory

So, dare to let me take care of you
Let me love you
Let me love others through you
Look, I am making everything new
I am giving you a new heart
A new heart for a new season
Make discoveries with me

Heart to Heart

I have one thing on my heart
That you should seek me
and come before my presence
with an undivided heart
Let nothing stop you
Do not bring excuses
Do not wait

The time is now
The time is here

I am calling on you
Your spirit can sense it
and is longing for my presence
But your soul is hesitating
Your soul is wounded
And your thoughts are bound
in vain imaginations
I am the only one who can set you free

I am the only one who can heal you
Do not hesitate
What do you have to lose
I am waiting, waiting in love
Listen to my voice
Follow it
Dare to follow your heart
Because it knows the call
It knows where it is pleasant to be
It knows where it belongs
The time is now
The time is here

I do not condemn you
I have never done so
I release you
Set you free
Receive

The time is now
The time is here

In me there is fullness of joy
In me there is perfect harmony
I am longing to share it with you
Let me embrace you
My presence is casting out all fear

And the time is now
The time is here
Because I am here
Where you are

In the Eyes of God

I wish you could see yourself
as I see you
Because I see a lot of possibilities in you
You have gifts within you
gifts that I have placed there
Small seedlings that need to be watered
so that they are rooted and can come in full bloom

Dare to be loved by me
Then you will see them sprouting
Dare to hope
Then you will see them budding
Dare to live a life with me
Then you will see them blooming
And that blooming will never cease

Come to Me

Come to me, you who are thirsty
You who are longing for life
You who are crying for truth
Come to me with struggles and strife

Come to me, you who are longing
Who are longing for goodness
You who are struggling with your burden
Come to me, encounter my mildness

Come to me, you who are striving
You who have no strength
You who are fighting in pain
I bore the cross for you

Because in me is the fountain of life
I will always be close
So, let go of your burdens
I will give you the garments of joy

My Mirror

Will you be my mirror
Be the one who reflects my light
so that it can enlighten a darkened mind
so that it can set people free

Will you be my mirror
Will you make sure to be
in the right position in relationship with me
so that you can reflect my glory
My light of truth
My love

Then you must always make sure to be cleansed
and be in right position
Then I can use you like a laser
to bring healing and clarity
cleansing and life

Will you be my mirror

The Paths of the Lord

Will you walk on my paths
My paths are marked
When you reach one mark
You will see the next a little further away
But you will have to start walking
You will have to trust me
that I am leading you right
I have a path just for you
It is *your* path
No one has trod on it before
No one will walk on it after you

It takes you upwards and downwards
onwards and around
There are places you must climb
There are places you must bow down
There are places with rumbling waterfalls
and places with total stillness

I see and know you
You must trust that I know
what you always need
I know when you need challenges
I know when you need rest
I know when you need vision
I know when you need a hiding place

There are many brooks along my path
Places where you can quench your thirst
but then you will have to bow down
Only then it will be possible to drink
The path also passes by restful waters
And green meadows

So, come
Turn off the road
And dare to walk on my paths
Your path is waiting for you

In the Father's Breast Pocket

Lift your eyes
Look what I will show you
I the Father, am bowing down
and am lifting you up
in my strong hand
There is plenty of room
in my hand

I am lifting you up
And putting you carefully
In my left breast pocket
Close to my heart
so that you can hear it beating
so that you can listen
to my visions and
what I am longing for
When our hearts beat together
Then you are ready
for sharing with others
my innermost thoughts
because then we are one

Your Papa

Will you let me be your papa
Will you let me wipe your tears
Will you let me hear your angry cries
Do you to dare to trust me

Do you dare to take the chance that I love you
That I love you as you are
Do you dare to throw off your mask
Letting me see how vulnerable you are

I am standing with open arms
To take you into my embrace
I will rock you slowly to the beat of my heart
And tell you that I love you so much

Soaring

I have called you to soar
on the wings I have given you
If you dare to throw yourself out
from your safe nest
You shall sense that my winds are carrying you
My winds are lifting you up
to my throne
From there I will show you my Kingdom
you will see as I see

Dare to trust that my winds will carry you
When you dance for me
you describe who I am
You are painting a picture of me
With your movements
Let me inspire you
for I am the source of the dance

Right Element

I went for a walk along the beach
There I discovered a stone
That rested by itself
I lifted it up and felt it
and knew it belonged
in another element

I knew that in that stone
there were hidden treasures
The stone belonged in the water
I put it down and saw at once
the quality emerged
as it lay in the water
and sparkled in the sunshine

You are that stone
If you want, I can lift you up
And place you in my Kingdom
in the Living water
There your beauty and your gifts
will come into your own
In my glorious light
in my presence
you can shine
There you will be safe

Masterpiece

It feels like your life is crushed
When you look down you see a lot of pieces
pieces of glass lying in a heap
a life gone to pieces

But I, I see possibilities
to make a beautiful glass painting
You have so many beautiful colors inside of you
They shall create the most beautiful picture

I will melt the pieces together
using my Holy fire and love
When the painting is finished you will radiate
when my light shines on you

So, let me finish my work
I am the Master
I see where the pieces are fitting
Place your life in my creative hand

Rejected

I want you to know that you
you are not rejected by me
You have never been rejected by me
The lie about everybody rejecting you
let it be broken
because I was and am with you

I was rejected for you
that you should be spared
You are accepted and
so much loved by me
Receive my truth about you
Let it fill you
Let it set you free

Forsaken

Why have you forsaken me
I said to my Father
as I hung on the cross
He had to
So that you should never be forsaken
I felt the darkness
the emptiness and despair
the heaviness of forsakenness

You were and are never forsaken by me
I am always by your side
When the enemy is whispering lies
«You are alone»
Then you shall declare
«It is a lie
He is always with me»
I, who am the Truth
have said so
I am with you

Okay to Cry

It is tough
You want to cry
It is hard
You just want to give up
You feel the tears coming
A voice from the past says
– Do not cry now
– Boys do not cry

You swallow every tear
Your tears are making a lump
It would have been so good
to have it removed
express the hurt and pain

Then you hear another voice
A mild and quiet voice
– It is okay to cry now
My son Jesus, also cried
so why not you
I have room for all your tears
Let me embrace you
so that you can cry all your tears
towards my heart
Then I can come with my comfort
You can come to me for strength
and the help you need
First you must know
it is okay to cry now

Water and Fire

Your own little ice age is soon over
Your own little ice age is soon at an end
The ice you have covered around your heart
is soon history and that ice will be broken

In your inside I have made my residence
In your spirit The Holy Spirit lives
who has melted from the inside that ice
that has subdued you with a harsh hand

In your heart the water will rise
It will fill your heart up to the brim
My Holy Spirit will fill every chamber
It will rise to the top of your heart

When the water reaches the ceiling
then my Spirit can catch fire and will melt
down the ice that encloses you
It will evaporate every tear you shed

When my fire has melted all ice
when there are no ice grains left
Then my Spirit and Fire can work
on your soul and body, my friend

So, let me finish my work
Let me melt the last remains
You have so much good in front of you
Let your pain float away
Trust me because I love you the most

The Fire of the Lord

I am a consuming fire
You know the fire – you know what it does
It removes impurity
Go into my fire
stay there – dwell there
In my presence everything dies that is not of me

It is a time of pain and crying
and not joy
Will you take part and birth the baby?
Are you willing to know the pain during contractions?
Know the despair and cry out my pain?

I need you
your heart, your spirit
Tread into the fire and let the tears turn to vapor
The vapor becomes rain that waters the earth

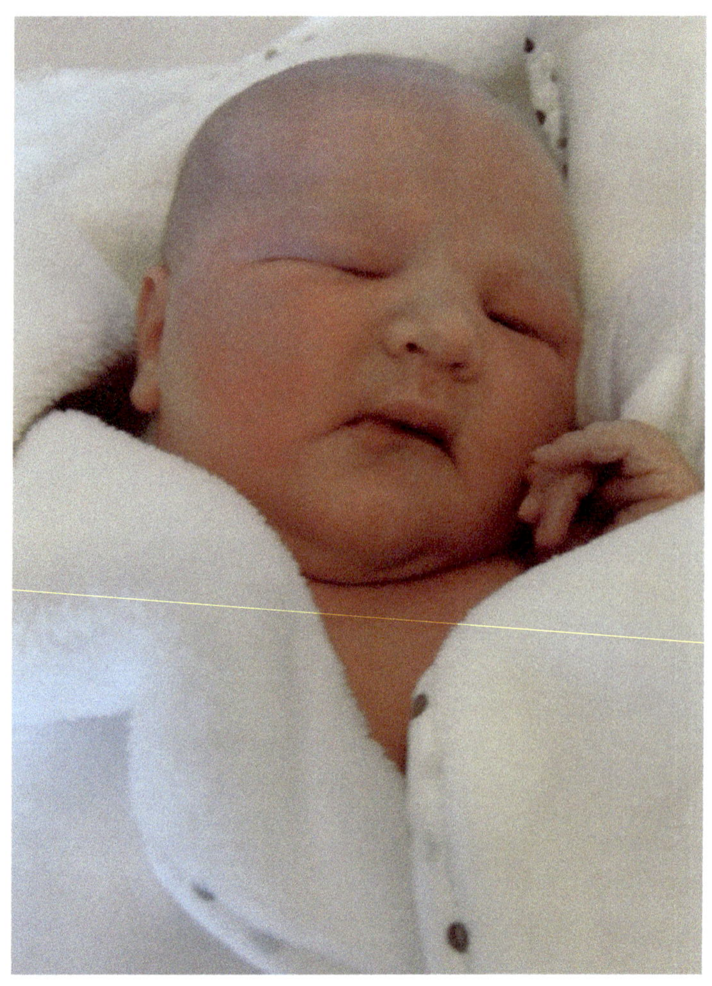

Birth

I came into being by a fusion
between my mother and father
Semen from my father
and egg from my mother made me
In wondrous ways and I became me
a unique person with many possibilities
Did I look mostly like my mother or father

Then came birth number two
God's seed, God's living word
melted together with my spirit in faith
and I received a new life, an eternal life
and even more possibilities
Now I could take after my heavenly Father

I have genes from my mother and my father
They have taken part in shaping me
But I also have genes from the living God
What dispositions do I let dominate me
Who do I want to resemble the most

A Father and a Daughter

A father is gone, and memories are flooding
They keep on pushing, they keep coming
Not all are good, the sad ones are coming too
from travels, from holidays, by car and boat and train
from infancy, from schooldays
from childhood home to dancing and singing
Big memories and small memories
Some with dimples and some that are grey
some have siblings in them
Tears running down a cheek
some are like small flowers
very pleasant to sniff at
Some are like roses with thorns
or like violets, blue as the sky

You can pick the one you wish for
pick the one you want
But remember you still are loved
by a Father who is eternal and great
You can always find his lap
if it is as a child or as a woman
He has always time, always room
You are the apple of his eye, to him you are special
His eyes delight in you, you bring joy to his heart
He is thinking about you
He is preparing a place for you

Let the sorrow have its place
but then let the joy take you along
Because you are alive, and you are you
You are made to rejoice, to dance around
to sing, to praise, to worship your God
his holy truth, his mighty Heavens

So, rejoice my daughter, rejoice in me
Let the tears flow, but remember, I love you

A Lost Son

Son
Hungry
I am hungry
Even the food of the pigs looks inviting
The hunger is gnawing
How did I get here!
How could I have been that stupid
I had such a nice time
I was loved by my father
I had everything I needed

Look at me now
Maybe I could go back
Work as a servant
Even the servants are like kings compared to this
Do I dare to go back
Do I dare to look my father in his eyes
I will perish here
I choose life before death

Father
Where are you my beloved son
Are you dead or alive
I am watching for you every day
I am hoping and yearning
Tomorrow you surely will be here
If you only knew how much I love you
It does not matter what you did

There
There you are
I will run and meet you
All is forgiven
You are my son and no servant
Let me embrace you
Let me have a party for you
Now my heart can rejoice
My son has come home

Two Fathers

Abraham went for a walk with his son
He had got an order from God during his prayers
He went with a heavy heart
while looking at his son
"God knows best, he knows what he is doing
He will answer the same if I ask him again"
Lose his son, could he do that
even sacrifice his son himself

But God is powerful, he can do anything
He had to do what the Lord had commanded
God could give his son back

Now the alter and the son was ready for his knife
But at the last second God stopped the man
and said: It is enough, I will give you another
An offering was chosen, a ram this time
and in his heart, there was a song
He had his son a second time

God thought and he knew—a substitutional lamb
Next time it happened, he would be the father
He had to sacrifice his son, he had to
His beloved, his only, he both could and would
The heart of God cried, he saw his son
He had to walk through death
There was no other way
Than the road of death out of love
He had to let go of his son
had to leave him, listen to his groans
had to listen to his pain
Sense it in his heart
But in the end, he would triumph
God would no longer be alone
His son would be back and had received his reward
God was once more together with his son

True Colors

The forest stands in flames
continuous new places catch fire
a dramatic change
almost like a fairy tale

A leaf hanging
just like others, just as green
suddenly becomes transformed
to flaming beauty

The likeness disappears
The mask is gone
What hid it is gone
every spot has disappeared

The time has come
to show who you are
Let all your gifts
come forth, your time is here

And when you like the leaf on the tree
are loosed from its hold
you can dance on the winds of God
You can be jubilant and free

Because for that the Lord has created you
He has taken away all the blame and shame
Now you can use your freedom
to rejoice in him

Frost Heave

The soil is moving
It is pushing and pulling
Stones that were deep down
is coming up
Things that were hidden
are coming up

The farmer that had cleared the field
Had to take a new round
The soil had to be cleared
to get good growth
In that way the soil is enriched
so that the harvest can be plentiful

Do we have stones in our lives
things that are hidden
things that we know nothing about
When we are coming into a new spring
things are beginning to happen
Things are moving inside of us

No use saying to yourself
There is nothing there
They will not go away
Best thing is to remove them
So that they do not hinder the growth
and the harvest can be plentiful

Prayer

Outstretched hands
Tears flowing
Laughter pealing
The guitar that is playing
The cries that are echoing
The sorrow like a hunger
The joy in a dance
Laughter without seizing
Silent sighs in distress
Cries from the heart with passion
Angry cries and wrath
High jumps in joy
A song to be sung
A heavy heart

All this can be called prayer
Your sincerity will be rewarded

The Strangest Thing

The son of God became human
How strange is that
Was conceived in a woman
A fetus so little and fragile
laid there and grew
in a woman's body
Knew the pain
as he came out and up

He got a smile
from the mouth of Mary
He was held close to her breast
A delightful moment
words that were whispered
a thank you up to God
«To think that you
just to me sent your message»

«To think that I am holding
a savior in my arms
To think that Gabriel said
that Jesus is your name
You shall be loved
I have given you my heart
So, from this moment
It will always be yours»

The Declaration of Love from the Bride

I will touch your face
you, who my soul loves
I want to see your smiling wrinkles
as you are smiling at me
Your beaming eyes that
are shining like the morning star
as thousands of stars
Those that see straight into my heart
Those that see my innermost dreams
my innermost longings

Your eyes are shining from love
I want to drown in them
My eyes are flowing
When I feel your love
It is melting and becomes a cascade
Of praise and worship
I am dancing in joy that my bridegroom
Is finding me worthy to be loved

I want to sit by your feet
And let your loving hands
Stroke my head
so that all my worries are melting away
and your peace is filling all of me

You are Holy no Matter What

Even when my tears are flowing
when the bridges are burning
when my powers are dwindling
when the liars are winning
You are holy no matter what

Even when the fights are coming
when the rain is pouring
when the pain is burning
the boat is heaving
You are holy no matter what

Even when friendships are ending
when the need is acute
when sleep does not come
when the bills are flowing
I will anyway say
You are holy no matter what

About the Author

Inger Marie Nordin began her Christian journey at 14 years of age, growing to hear God's voice after being baptized in the Spirit at 16. She moves in the gifts of teaching and prophecy—seeing the supernatural behind the natural—and enjoys ministering at her church, singing in the Spirit and taking photographs of God's creation. Inger began writing poetry as the Lord ministered to her during a difficult time in her life and is now led to pass it on to others. She makes her home in Oslo, Norway, and gives thanks to God for her daughter, son-in-law and two grandsons.

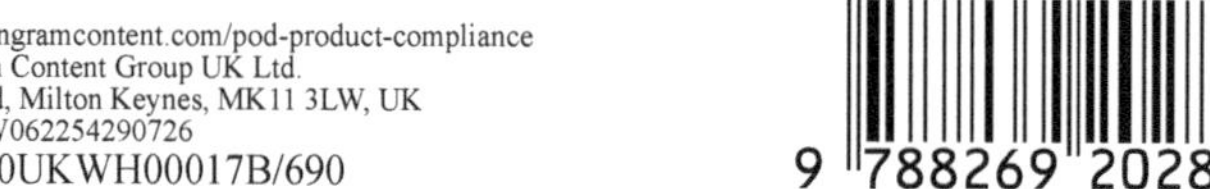
www.ingramcontent.com/pod-product-compliance
Ingram Content Group UK Ltd.
Pitfield, Milton Keynes, MK11 3LW, UK
UKHW062254290726
14090UKWH00017B/690

9 788269 202847